THE STORY OF JONAH

Adapted from *The Book of Jonah*

By Pamela Broughton ♦ Illustrated by Roberta Collier

A GOLDEN BOOK • NEW YORK

Western Publishing Company, Inc., Racine, Wisconsin 53404

Copyright © 1986 by Western Publishing Company, Inc. Illustrations copyright © 1986 by Roberta Collier.
All rights reserved. Printed in the U.S.A. No part of this book may be reproduced or copied in any form without written
permission from the publisher. GOLDEN®, GOLDEN & DESIGN®, A GOLDEN BOOK®, and A LITTLE GOLDEN BOOK®
are trademarks of Western Publishing Company, Inc. Library of Congress Catalog Card Number: 85-81160   ISBN 0-307-02081-9
CDEFGHIJ

The Lord said to Jonah, "Go to the great city of Nineveh. Tell the people there that I have heard of their wickedness. If they do not change their ways, Nineveh will be destroyed."

But Jonah rose up and fled to Joppa. There he found a ship bound for another city. He paid his fare and went on board.

The Lord caused a great storm to come up. The sailors were afraid. Each man called on his own god to save him.

Jonah was asleep in the hold of the ship.
The captain came to Jonah and said, "How can you sleep?
Get up and call on your god! Perhaps your god will save us."

The sailors rolled dice to see who was to blame for
the storm. The blame fell to Jonah.

Then Jonah told them, "My God is the Lord God of heaven, who made the sea and the dry land. This storm has come upon you because of me. Pick me up and throw me into the sea."

The sailors did not want Jonah to drown because of them. But the storm grew worse.

The men begged Jonah's God for mercy. Then they threw Jonah into the sea.

The sea grew calm, and the sailors prayed to Jonah's God.

The Lord God sent a huge fish to swallow Jonah.
Jonah was inside the fish for three days and three nights.

Then Jonah prayed to the Lord.
"I called out to the Lord, and He answered me."

"You bring me up from the depths, O Lord! I will do what I have promised."

Then the Lord commanded the great fish to cough up
Jonah onto dry land.

The word of the Lord came to Jonah a second time, saying, "Go to the great city of Nineveh, and say what I shall tell you."

So Jonah went to Nineveh.

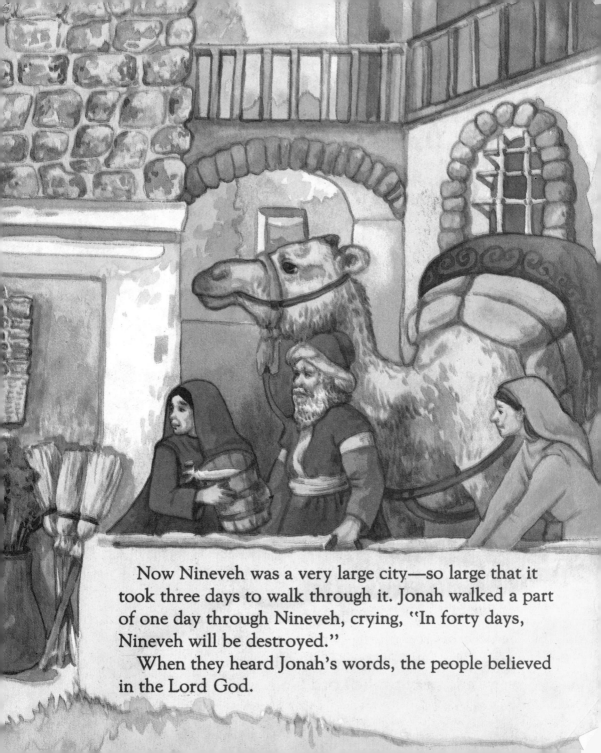

Now Nineveh was a very large city—so large that it took three days to walk through it. Jonah walked a part of one day through Nineveh, crying, "In forty days, Nineveh will be destroyed."

When they heard Jonah's words, the people believed in the Lord God.

When Jonah's words reached the King of Nineveh, he put off his royal robes and put on rough clothes. He ordered all the people of the city to stop their wicked ways and pray to the Lord God.

When the Lord God saw that the people turned away from wickedness, He did not destroy the city.

And Jonah was angry. He thought his trip to Nineveh had been useless. "This is what I was afraid of," he complained. "This is why I wanted to flee."

Jonah went out of the city and built a shelter. He waited to see what would happen to Nineveh.

And the Lord God caused a plant to grow up, to
shade Jonah from the heat. Jonah was pleased.

But at dawn the next day, God sent a worm to kill the plant. Then God sent a scorching east wind.

The sun beat down on Jonah. He grew faint and begged God to let him die.

Then God said, "You felt sorry for the plant, which you did not raise or tend, and which lived only for a day and a night.

"Should I not then feel sorry for Nineveh, where there are so many people and animals, all of them My children?"